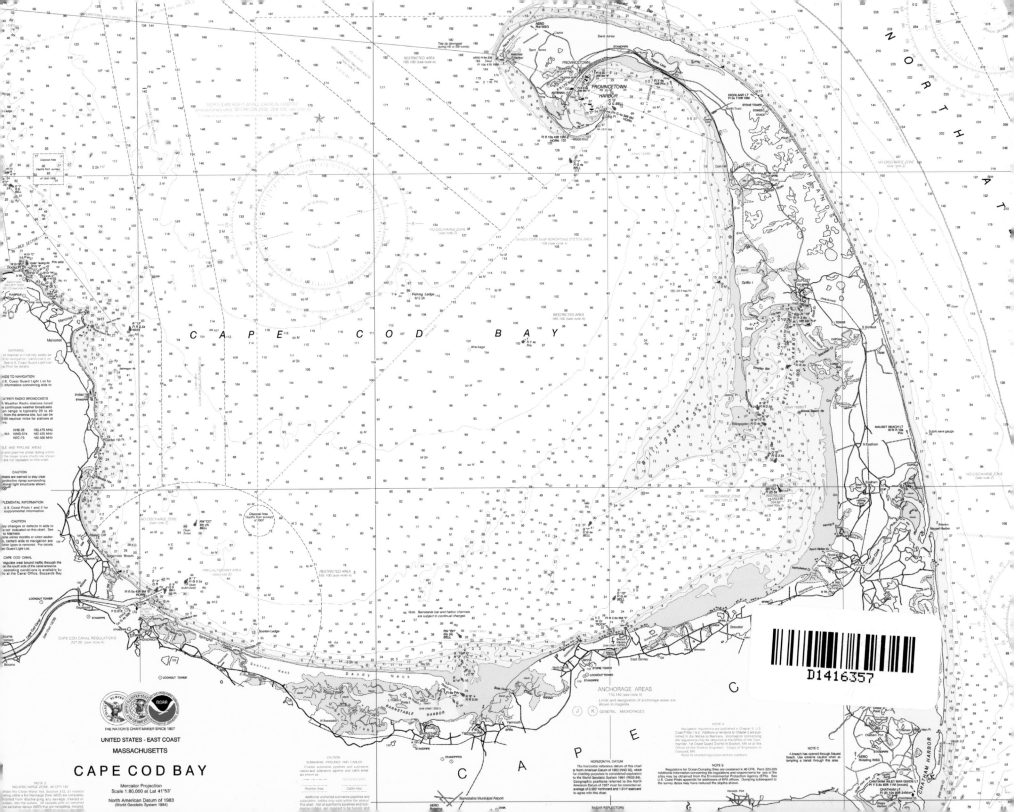

CAPE COD BAY

UNITED STATES - EAST COAST

MASSACHUSETTS

CAPE COD BAY

Mercator Projection
Scale 1:80,000 at Lat 41°53'

North American Datum of 1983
(World Geodetic System 1984)

D1416357

C is for Cape Cod

Exploring the Cape from A to Z

WRITTEN BY **CHRISTINA LAURIE**   PHOTOGRAPHS BY **STEVE HEASLIP**

April 26,
2015
To Dear Math Sarah!
your sweet Easter Bunny
Baby --- Maizie Elizabeth --
Blessings to you three ---
A fun story about the magic & beauty
of Cape Cod ---
Love, your friend, Maria xo

ISLANDPORT PRESS

Published by Islandport Press
P.O. Box 10
Yarmouth, Maine 04096
books@islandportpress.com
www.islandportpress.com

ISBN: 978-1-939017-13-0
Library of Congress Control Number: 2013955828
Printed in the USA by Versa Press

Dedicated to my seven grandchildren, who all love Cape Cod: Cooper, Will, Miles, Olivia, Trevor, Tate, and Beckett.—CHRISTINA

To Holly, Kate, Scott, Mom, and Dad for a lifetime of support for my photography.—STEVE

ONCE CALLED the "bare bended arm of Massachusetts," Cape Cod sticks out into the Atlantic Ocean from the otherwise rectangular state. This roughly eighty-mile-long spit of land has almost 560 miles of coastline. It was formed thousands of years ago by glacial ice which slowly receded to leave the arm-shaped sandbar, with Martha's Vineyard, Nantucket, and the Elizabeth Islands hanging off its southern shore like tear drops.

Surrounded by dangerous shoals, the peninsula boasts more than twenty lighthouses, dramatic beaches, and mild weather. Pockmarked with fresh water ponds, salt marshes, and cranberry bogs, it offers a wonderland retreat for summer visitors.

Painter Mary Moquin works under a dramatic sky at Sandy Neck Beach.

A is for Artists

Painters and potters, so many around.
A chain-saw sculptor can even be found.

AT THE END of the nineteenth century, artists arrived on the sand dunes of lower Cape Cod. They set up easels and beach chairs, opened their paint boxes, and re-created scenes along the shores and in quaint towns. The Cape still attracts creative people from all over the world. Dozens of art museums display art and artifacts, from Bourne to Provincetown.

Many painters, writers, musicians, sculptors, potters, photographers, and glassblowers make Cape Cod their home.

There's even a chain-saw sculptor on the Cape. The chain-saw sculptor chooses a stump or large piece of wood and begins with his noisy chain saw. To make tiny details like fur or feathers, he may use a smaller saw, chisel, sander, or grinder.

A is also for aquarium, Atlantic Ocean, the *Alvin*, algae, alewives, anemones, and appetite.

Lights from the Cape Cod Canal Railroad Bridge sparkle on a still winter morning, just before sunrise.

Bis for Bridges

To cross the canal,
take a bridge;
there are three!
For cars and trains,
for you and for me.

BEFORE THE CAPE COD CANAL was built, ships had to sail 165 miles around the peninsula, braving hidden rocks, strong currents, and pirates.

The canal, a man-made channel, cuts an opening between the Cape Cod peninsula and the mainland. It opened in 1914. The two bridges crossing over the canal had to pivot so that boats could pass. In 1935, the Army Corps of Engineers replaced them with two higher, larger bridges at Sagamore and Bourne. Spanning the 480-foot-wide, 17.4-mile-long Cape Cod Canal, these two highway bridges see more than 35 million vehicles cross every year.

The third bridge, built in 1910, is the Cape Cod Canal Railroad Bridge, rising 135 feet on steel towers.

B is also for baseball league, Barnstable County Fair, boardwalks, beach plum, barnacles, and bait.

Bog workers pull berries into a spigot, which draws them up through a sorting machine and into a waiting truck at the Jenkins family bog.

C is for Cranberries

Cape Cod's fruit,
bright red and round,
grows in sandy bogs
close to the ground.

CAPE COD CRANBERRIES are famous the world over, and many seasonal visitors take tours of the Cape's cranberry bogs.

Cranberries grow in full sunlight on low shrubs or trailing vines in wet, sandy sod called bogs. The Cape has just the right conditions needed to grow cranberries: lots of water, lots of sand, and four distinct seasons.

Because cranberries have little pockets of air inside, they float! So when the berries ripen, farmers flood the bogs with water, stirring it with a tool called an eggbeater to loosen the berries from the vines. The cranberries float to the surface and are gathered using a boom; then they are sucked up by a berry pump. Most of the Cape's cranberries are made into juice.

C is also for catboat, camping, Cape Cod Canal, crab, clam, cable, creeks, and codfish.

Beach grass bends in the wind over Sandy Neck Beach, facing Cape Cod Bay.

D is for Dunes

Rocks turn to sand
and become dunes
on the shore,
protecting the land
with beach grass galore.

SAND DUNES BEGAN as rocks millions of years ago. Wind, waves, and glaciers ground the rocks into tiny bits of sand, which formed high hills called sand dunes. Dunes are important to the Cape because they protect the inner land from storm waves that sweep the coast.

Each year, storms, wind, and tidal shifts change the shape of the dunes. Your favorite beach might look very different from one year to the next.

Long, thin beach grass grows in the dunes and holds the sand in place, protecting it from the harsh weather. However, walkers and beach vehicles, called dune buggies, can kill the grass, causing the dunes to wash away and slip into the ocean.

D is also for drawbridge, docks, ducks, dragonflies, dogwood, dogfish, and dove.

*Kayakers head out across
a flooded estuary
off Buttermilk Bay.*

E is for Estuary

Where freshwater meets salt,
sea creatures breed.
Let's try to give them
the care that they need.

CAPE COD SITS ON a sandbar on top of rock, pushed there by prehistoric glaciers. When the ice melted, basins formed around the edges of the Cape. These basins filled with freshwater and sediments flowing down from groundwater and streams in the hills and mountains. The freshwater mixes with salty ocean water brought in by the tide, creating estuaries.

Plants, shellfish, and small animals live and breed in these estuaries. These plants and animals cannot live anywhere else.

Estuaries are sensitive, and man-made pollution can be very harmful to them. Many groups research estuarine life on the Cape. Scientists study what people can do to keep water clean and habitats healthy. We can help, too, by being conscious of what we do with our water and trash.

E is also for eelgrass, engineers, ecosystem, eel, egret, and erosion.

Josh Raia, left, and Ernie Eldredge offload fish at the dock at Stage Harbor in Chatham.

F is for Fisherman

Wide trawlers
with fish in their belly
slide into docks.
Oh, my! They are smelly!

BECAUSE THE CAPE is surrounded by water, one of the largest industries next to tourism is the $14 million a year fishing business. Many commercial fishermen operate their boats in the Georges Bank, about sixty miles offshore. Georges Bank is a shoal—a plain or flat area lying in shallow waters that is not as deep as the rest of the ocean. Cold waters from Canada mix with warm waters coming from Mexico, creating rich fishing grounds. Fishermen search for cod, flounder, pollock, fluke, and herring.

Sportfishermen look for swordfish, tuna, mackerel, and white marlin off Cape Cod waters. There's even a Monster Shark Tournament every summer in Oak Bluffs on Martha's Vineyard, to catch the largest shark in the waters surrounding the Cape.

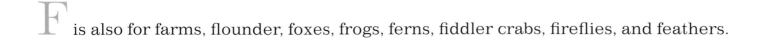

F is also for farms, flounder, foxes, frogs, ferns, fiddler crabs, fireflies, and feathers.

A glassblower uses a torch to heat a glass hand sculpture at the McDermott Glass Studio in Sandwich.

G is for Glassblowing

With red, puffy cheeks
and a steady hand,
the glassblower creates
jars and vases from sand.

IN 1825, A MAN named Deming Jarves made a decision that would change the town of Sandwich forever: He opened the Boston & Sandwich Glass Company, brought in the best glassblowers he could find, and started making beautiful products from glass.

Now, Cape Cod is famous for its glass. Many glass companies and museums give tours so you can watch glassblowers at work. You will see a wide variety of colorful blown-glass bowls, Christmas decorations, plates, and *witch balls*— hollow balls said to ward off evil spirits.

Glass is made from sand, but usually not from ordinary beach sand. To make clear, pure glass, you need pure quartz silica. The silica is heated until it turns into a liquid, and then it is either machine-molded or made into different shapes by blowing air through a long glass tube.

G is also for gristmills, gulls, grackle, grape vines, Gay Head, and glacial rocks.

A hermit crab navigates the waters off Sandy Neck Beach in Barnstable.

H is for Hermit Crab

A young hermit crab naturally knows to change its house each time it grows.

BRAIDED TRAILS OVER low-tide mudflats indicate tiny hermit crabs are nearby! You might not see one, since hermits are shy. When startled, they retract into their shell or quickly dig a hole and crawl in.

To protect its soft, curved abdomen, the hermit crab finds an empty snail shell and moves in, securing itself in place with its hooked hind claws. Four pincher claws help it dig into the sand, and two larger, hard nippers grab and hold its food.

As the crab grows, it seeks a larger, movable house. When a bigger shell becomes available, hermit crabs gather around and line up, from largest to smallest. When the biggest crab moves into the new shell, the second biggest moves into the newly vacated shell, and so on down the line.

H is also for herring, haddock, horseshoe crabs, heron, Heritage Museum, and Hoxie House.

Crowds gather at the Camp Meeting Association grounds in Oak Bluffs to view the gingerbread cottages decorated for Illumination Night.

I is for Islands

Two famous islands are just a short hop. Tourists flock out there to bike, swim, and shop.

MARTHA'S VINEYARD is a scenic ferry ride from Falmouth or Hyannis. Its Methodist campground in Oak Bluffs is surrounded by brightly colored houses with gingerbread decorations. In August, islanders celebrate "Illumination Night" by decorating the houses surrounding the campground with multicolored lanterns.

Most of Nantucket, which can be reached by ferry or plane, is a natural preservation area, including soft, sandy beaches. About ten thousand people live on the island, which is fourteen miles long and about four miles wide.

A third island called Billingsgate was one of the places the Pilgrims landed in 1620. Because of erosion, the sixty-acre community on the island was abandoned in 1912, and soon disappeared into the ocean. All that remains is a sandbar, visible only at low tide.

I is also for Indian pipes, ice farms, invertebrates, insects, and icebergs.

Moon jellies swirl around an exhibit at the Cape Cod Museum of Natural History in Brewster.

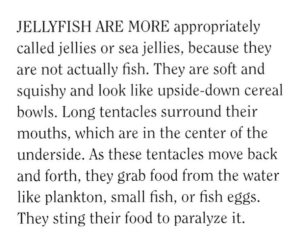

J is for Jellyfish

Jellies of the sea
have no bones and no brain.
These critters are pretty
but can sure be a pain!

JELLYFISH ARE MORE appropriately called jellies or sea jellies, because they are not actually fish. They are soft and squishy and look like upside-down cereal bowls. Long tentacles surround their mouths, which are in the center of the underside. As these tentacles move back and forth, they grab food from the water like plankton, small fish, or fish eggs. They sting their food to paralyze it.

Jellies are 95 percent water, and are brainless, bloodless, and boneless. They live in colonies in the open sea but drift to warm waters during the summer. They swim by a series of rhythmical pulses, which are almost like heartbeats.

Jellies can be as long as a house or as small as a pin. It's safer not to touch them, because some can give you a painful sting.

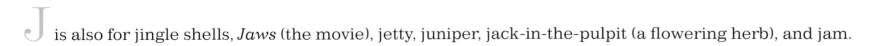

J is also for jingle shells, *Jaws* (the movie), jetty, juniper, jack-in-the-pulpit (a flowering herb), and jam.

A kiteboarder gets ready to test the wind at Corporation Beach in Dennis.

K is for Kite-boarding

On some sandy beaches when the surf is so high, folks riding kiteboards seem to touch the sky.

KITEBOARDING is an exciting sport for windy days off the shores of the Cape and nearby islands. People strap their feet onto a board, tie their bodies into a four-rope harness attached to a forty-foot-wide kite, and skim over the water. Some jump as high as forty feet and even do somersaults.

The kite can rise ninety feet into the air, pulling the boarder as fast as thirty-five miles an hour. *Kitemares* are stories boarders tell of the dangerous times they have experienced.

Kiteboarding is an outgrowth of surfboarding and windsurfing, which came to Cape Cod in the 1960s, but is more dangerous because of the high speeds.

K is also for kale, kayak, King's Highway, kettle ponds, kingfisher, and kelp.

A spring snowstorm coats the area around Nauset Light with a heavy, wet snow.

L is for Lighthouse

Tall lighthouses,
slender and white,
guide sailing vessels
on a foggy night.

CAPE COD HAS EIGHTEEN lighthouses on the mainland and ten on the islands. These lighthouses symbolize safety and security for sailors, boaters, and fishermen from Bourne to Provincetown. Their beams can extend up to thirty miles out to sea.

The oldest—and tallest—lighthouse on Cape Cod is Highland Light in Truro. It's sometimes called the Cape Cod Light. Built in 1797, the lighthouse sat near the edge of Truro's steep cliffs. As the cliffs eroded, the lighthouse got closer and closer to the edge! In 1996, the lighthouse was moved back more than 450 feet.

Lighthouse beacons were originally lit by wood fires, candles, or oil. Lighthouse keepers lived in the lighthouses, keeping the candles lit, or replenishing the oil three or four times every twenty-four hours. Today, most lighthouses are run by electricity.

L is also for lobster, Long Pond, lichens, loons, ladder shell, lugworms, and least tern.

The swordfish weathervane points the way as clouds thicken over the Godfrey Windmill in Chatham.

M is for Mills

Grinding wheels use wind for power as round millstones turn grain to flour.

GRISTMILLS WERE ONCE popular along Cape waterways. Wooden blades, turned by wind or water, caused two large round stones, called millstones, to turn. The millstones ground the grain, making flour from wheat or corn.

The Cape's oldest windmill, built in 1680, stands in Eastham, ready for visitors to explore. It wasn't always there; it was built in Plymouth and ferried on a raft across Cape Cod Bay to Eastham.

The oldest functioning windmill in the country stands atop Mill Hill on the island of Nantucket. Built in 1746 from pegs and wood from wrecked ships, the Old Mill stands fifty feet tall and has four thirty-foot blades. In winter, the blades are placed on the ground to protect them from the harsh ocean winds and storms.

M is also for marine biology, mollusks, Monarch butterflies, mussels, marsh grass, mudflats, and mackerel.

N is for National Seashore

The National Seashore on Cape Cod's outer arm keeps beaches and birds sheltered from harm.

MUCH OF THE SANDY outer edge of Cape Cod is part of the Cape Cod National Seashore. In 1961, 44,000-plus acres of sand dunes, forests, and open land were rescued from the Cape building boom by a law supported by President John F. Kennedy. No homes or businesses may be built in this area. The land is preserved forever.

The National Seashore has two visitor centers, six stunning beaches, three bike trails, and many hiking and walking trails. It is also home to a few endangered species, including a four-inch gray bird called the piping plover. During nesting season, plovers lay tiny sand-colored eggs along the shore. These nesting areas are closed to visitors to make sure the camouflaged eggs can safely hatch.

N is also for Nauset Cliffs, nuthatch, night herons, Nashaquitsa Cliffs, Naushon Island, and neap tides.

White Crest Beach in Wellfleet is popular with surfers, boogie-boarders, walkers, and sand castle makers.

O is for Ocean

SEVERAL BODIES OF WATER surround the arm of the Cape. The cold Atlantic Ocean stretches along the forearm, or eastern, edge. To the south is Nantucket Sound. In the armpit between the peninsula and the mainland, Buzzards Bay is protected by the curve of the Cape. The body of water on the inside arm of the Cape is called Cape Cod Bay.

During the summer months, sailing, kayaking, and canoeing are popular in the warmer, calmer waters of these bays. On the rougher, colder ocean side, people kiteboard, water-ski, surf, boogie-board, and fish. Other enjoyable beach pastimes include sunbathing, searching for shells or sea glass, and dog-walking.

Swim, build sand castles, collect shells or sail. With water on all sides, a vacation can't fail!

O is also for oleander, Outermost House, osprey, owl, oysters, and orchestra.

A winter sky breaks open to the sun over Provincetown, as seen from MacMillan Wharf.

P is for Provincetown

At the sandy tip
of the Cape's curled arm,
bright houses and shops
show off P'town charm.

AT THE SICKLE-SHAPED TIP of the Cape is charming Provincetown, where the Mayflower first anchored. The Pilgrims traded rum for venison and corn. They didn't stay long because there was too much sand and too little grass for farming and grazing. They sailed farther up the coast to settle at Plymouth Rock.

In the early 1700s, a fishing village was established at Provincetown. Tiny houses were built close together as protection from the occasional French pirates who looted the village. Today some of these houses still stand along the tiny, one-way streets that meander through town.

In the 1700s and 1800s, whaling was the big trade, but today Provincetown is known for its theater, writing, and art colonies. Artists come from all over the world to live and work in this charming seaside town.

P is also for peepers, Pilgrim Monument, porpoise, pine, poison ivy, periwinkles, and presidents.

A quahog casts a shadow along Keyes Beach in Hyannis.

Q is for Quahog

THE QUAHOG *(KO-HOG)* is one of several different kinds of clams, and can live as long as thirty years. The name comes from the Indian word *poquauhock*, meaning horse fish. Native Americans used the inner purple shell or *wampum* as money or jewelry. Each line on the outer shell signifies one year of life; count the lines to see how long the clam has lived!

Quahogs have a hard oval shell and a short neck, and live just below the sand's surface at the edge of a beach or mudflat. They burrow into the sand or mud, leaving a small hole. When digging for quahogs, you must dig up the sand around the hole until you find it. Some people dig clams with special rakes, but others use their feet, a technique called treading.

The quahog is a type of clam; its shell is hard and white. If you find one on the beach, it may be closed up tight!

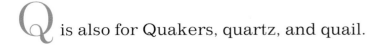

Q is also for Quakers, quartz, and quail.

Trains also carry freight on and off the Cape. This Mass Coastal train, nicknamed the Trash Train, carries rubbish from the Cape to a waste-to-energy plant on the mainland.

R is for Railroad

Running the rails, trains come to the Cape, giving city folks a way to escape!

TRAINS FIRST CONNECTED the mainland to Cape Cod in the mid-1800s and ran all the way to Provincetown by 1873. But once the car bridges over the canal were built, people drove instead, and the passenger trains stopped running.

Today the former railroads are being put to use again. A section of old train bed from North Falmouth to Woods Hole was turned into the seven-mile Shining Sea Bikeway (named for Katharine Lee Bates's poem, "America the Beautiful"). The twenty-six-mile Cape Cod Rail Trail meanders past salt marshes, cranberry bogs, and beaches as it travels from East Harwich to Wellfleet.

In 1999 the Cape Cod Central Railroad, from Hyannis to Buzzards Bay, was revived into a two-hour tourist trip along the Cape Cod Canal. In 2013, the CapeFlyer started up, carrying passengers once more from Boston to Hyannis.

R is for riprap, red tide, Revolutionary War, rugosa rose, raccoons, and rabbits.

S is for Seals

Smooth, shiny seals with eyes of brown bask in the sun and frolic around.

FUR-FOOTED SEALS come to the warm Cape waters each summer to fish and sunbathe. Two kinds of seals live in the Cape waters: harbor and gray seals. Intelligent and playful, they have eyes that can see both above and below the water. They can hold their breath for up to two hours. Their favorite food is fish, which they swallow whole, and shellfish, which they crush with their back molars.

If you don't spy a seal in the sea, you can always visit the two harbor seals that live at the Woods Hole Science Aquarium, a part of NOAA (National Oceanic and Atmospheric Administration). Five-year-old Bumper is blind, and his lively buddy LuSeal keeps him company. Both do tricks for visitors twice a day at feeding time.

S is for sharks, salt marsh, sand dollars, scrimshaw, seaweed, sea glass, and saltbox houses.

A box turtle searches for shade on a hot summer day near the woods in Barnstable.

T is for Turtles

Sea turtles come
to eat lots of jellies,
swimming north
to fill their bellies.

SEA TURTLES LEAVE their homes in the tropics and migrate north to Cape Cod Bay in warmer weather to eat jellyfish. As winter approaches, sea turtles normally head back south—but it doesn't always go according to plan!

As the ocean cools in the fall, the cold water stuns the turtles, and they cannot feed, dive, breathe, digest, or excrete. Volunteers and staff at a Massachusetts Audubon sanctuary, in Wellfleet Bay, rescue these "cold-stunned" turtles. After a recovery period in an aquarium, they are flown to warmer waters and released.

Cape Cod has freshwater turtles as well. The diamondback terrapin lives in estuaries and salt marshes. Look for painted, snapping, or the rare spotted turtle in ponds; box turtles can be seen in fields and forests.

T is also for tourists, train bridge, tugboat, terns, trails, tide pools, theaters, tent caterpillars, and termites.

Viewed from atop the Bourne Bridge, a Coast Guard patrol boat zips through the Cape Cod Canal.

U is for US Coast Guard

From boats and from planes, the Coast Guard will stand to guard and protect waters 'round the land.

THE UNITED STATES Coast Guard's ships and planes protect the New England coastline. For hundreds of years on Cape Cod, people have warned ships of the rocky coastline. Men ventured out during storms in small boats to rescue sailors and fishermen while their wives waited at home with warm blankets and hot tea.

There are several modern Coast Guard stations on Cape Cod, from a small station on Martha's Vineyard to the Cape Cod Air Station, a large base which lies in Mashpee, Bourne, and Sandwich. The Coast Guard conducts search-and-rescue missions, patrols the waterways, maintains aids to navigation, and helps to protect living marine resources.

If you are sitting on the beach, you might see a Coast Guard boat in the surf or spot a helicopter flying along the shoreline. Look for the signature red stripe!

U is also for urchins, undersea, and undertow.

Riders spin around on the popular and historic Flying Horses Carousel in Oak Bluffs, Martha's Vineyard.

V is for Vacationers

From residents to presidents, from far away and near, it's the sun, sand, and dunes that bring vacationers here.

CAPE COD, WITH A 220,000 year-round population, is one of the most sought-after retreats for people from all over the world. Vacationers come from as far away as Fiji, Japan, Iceland, and Australia.

The first tourists came by stagecoach to little village inns along the main roads. Later people arrived by train. Today cars cross the Bourne and Sagamore bridges, bringing millions of tourists to the Cape.

Even US presidents vacation here. In 1890, Grover Cleveland lived in Bourne at "Gray Gables," calling it the summer White House. Hyannis Port became the summer White House for John F. Kennedy and his brother, Attorney General Robert Kennedy. President Bill Clinton and his wife, Hillary Rodham Clinton, have vacationed on Martha's Vineyard, as have President Barack Obama and his family.

V is also for Vikings, violets, village green, voles, and vertebrates.

A humpback whale frolics for a crowded whale-watch boat about fifteen miles north of Provincetown.

W is for Whales

Whales migrate from north to south along the outer shore. They rise to breathe, then dive back down to fish or play some more.

WHALING WAS AN IMPORTANT industry on Cape Cod, especially on Nantucket, in the eighteenth and nineteenth centuries. Whales were hunted for meat and raw materials, including oil for lamps, *baleen* (rows of plates that look like the teeth of a comb), and *ambergris* (a perfume ingredient from the intestines of sperm whales). Millions of whales were killed, finally forcing a ban on whaling in 1986 by the International Whaling Commission.

Today whales contribute to a different industry: tourism! Boats take visitors on whale-watching trips to see these giant mammals as they breach, roll, skim-feed, and dive. Whales are very social animals and often play around boats. In the waters off Cape Cod, you might see minke, fin, sei, and humpback whales, and even the rare North Atlantic right whale.

W is also for Wampanoag Indians, wildflowers, witches, wharf, wind turbines, and whelks.

The Cape Cod Symphony performs at their annual Pops in the Park Concert in Orleans. Can you spot the xylophone?

X is for Xylophone

Music on the Cape is a natural affair. The symphony performs in the open air.

CAPE COD HAS MANY cultural organizations, including the Cape Cod Symphony Orchestra, which features a xylophone. Made up of about seventy-five musicians who live all over the Cape, the orchestra performs at the Barnstable Performing Arts Center in Hyannis. In the summer, outdoor concerts are held in Orleans and Falmouth.

The symphony conducts education programs in the Cape schools, and also supports the Cape Cod Conservatory of Music and Arts, which offers music, instrument, and dance classes for students and adults.

Many town bands perform summer evening concerts in music shells or sheds on village greens. From chamber music to rock, folk to jazz, you can hear it all on the Cape!

X is also for xerophytes (shore plants) and *Xanthocephalus xanthocephalus* (yellow-headed blackbird).

The Cotuit Mosquito Yacht Club Opti fleet takes to the waters of Cotuit Bay.

Y is for Yacht

Yachts and yawls
fly over the sea,
white sails flapping
in the breeze so free.

A YACHT IS A LIGHT, fast boat used for pleasure or racing. A yawl is a sailboat with two masts, with the smaller sail located behind the steering mechanism.

Sailing is one of the most popular pastimes of Cape Codders, and boats of all kinds can be seen from May to October. Small sunfish and sailfish compete with kayaks and canoes as they move through tributaries and marshes. Large yachts and motorboats whisk across larger lakes and bays. Small Beetle Cats (catboats) and lightning boats race on Buzzards Bay and Cape Cod Bay all summer.

You can learn more about sailboats and Cape Cod's boating history at the Cape Cod Maritime Museum in Hyannis, or experience it yourself on a tall ship sailing cruise on one of the Black Dog Tall Ships in Martha's Vineyard.

Y is also for Yankee Candle, yellow jackets, yarn, Yarmouth, yellowlegs (a shorebird), and yellow perch.

A right whale skim-feeds on Cape Cod Bay, using its baleen to capture zooplankton.

Z is for Zooplankton

Drifting on the ocean
in currents blue-green,
these little creatures
are too small to be seen.

MINUSCULE ONE-CELLED animals called zooplankton drift on currents near the surface of the ocean. They are an important food source for animals, both around Cape Cod and around the world.

Zooplankton are animal varieties of plankton (from a Greek word meaning "wandering"), which are mainly invertebrates (without skeletons). Although most zooplankton are too small to see, some kinds, like krill, are several inches in length. Krill is the main food that whales swallow.

Plankton are at the beginning of the food chain and make up the largest food mass in the ocean. Whales are at the top of the ocean's food chain, and eat thousands of pounds of zooplankton every day!

Z is also for zinnia, zoo, and zoophyte (plantlike animal).

ABOUT THE AUTHOR:

An internationally best-selling poet, **Christina Laurie** presents workshops, poetry readings, and seminars throughout New England. Her poems and haiku have appeared in magazines, anthologies, and periodicals across the United States, England, Canada, and Japan. Christina Laurie's first book, *Seasons Rising: A Collection of Haiku*, was published in 2011. She is the author of a memoir, two adult books on biblical characters, and a chapbook of inspirational insights, *Inspiration Interludes* (whose funds benefit the National League of American Pen Women). She lives, writes, swims, bikes, gardens, and kayaks on Cape Cod.

ABOUT THE PHOTOGRAPHER:

Steve Heaslip is the chief photographer for the *Cape Cod Times*. He has been a National Press Photographers Association regional and national clip contest winner, and was named New England Newspaper and Press Association Photographer of the Year in 2001 and 2005. His photographs have been in two exhibitions, and have appeared in *National Geographic*, *Life*, *Time*, *Newsweek*, the *New York Times*, and *Yankee*. Originally from Rochester, New York, he lives in Barnstable and has been photographing Cape Cod since the 1980s.

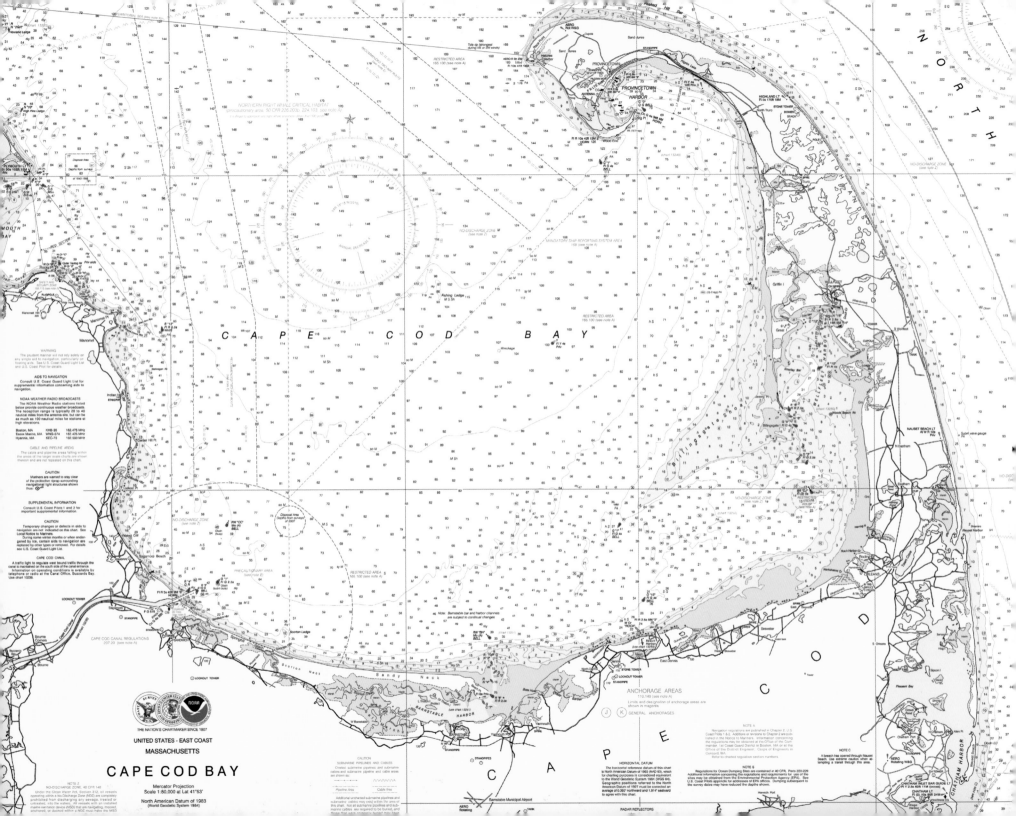

CAPE COD BAY

UNITED STATES - EAST COAST

MASSACHUSETTS

Mercator Projection
Scale 1:80,000 at Lat 41°53'

North American Datum of 1983
(World Geodetic System 1984)